FLASH AND FRIENDS ACTIVITY BOOK

Puzzles, Coloring Pages and Writing
For Kids who Love Horses!
Created by Natalie Bright

http://www.nataliebright.com
All rights reserved. Copyright NKB Books, LLC (2019)
Print ISBN 978-1-7331064-0-5

Disclaimer.

All rights reserved. No part of this book or this book as a whole may be used, reproduced or transmitted in any form or by any means, electronic, mechanical, photocopying, recording, scanning, or by an information storage and retrieval system, or transmitted by email without written permission from the author, except in the case of brief quotations embodied in critical articles and reviews. This book is for entertainment purposes only. The views express are those of the author alone.

For any inquiries regarding this book, please email: natalie@nataliebright.com

NKB BOOKS LLC
Canyon, Texas

In collaboration with
Christie Shippy Head, Flash's Owner/Trainer
Steven Raymond and Donavan Johnson, Original Puzzle Pages and Page Art
Cover Photograph by Lacy Johnston Photography
Cover Design by Steven Raymond
Layout Design & Formatting by Carpe Diem Publishers

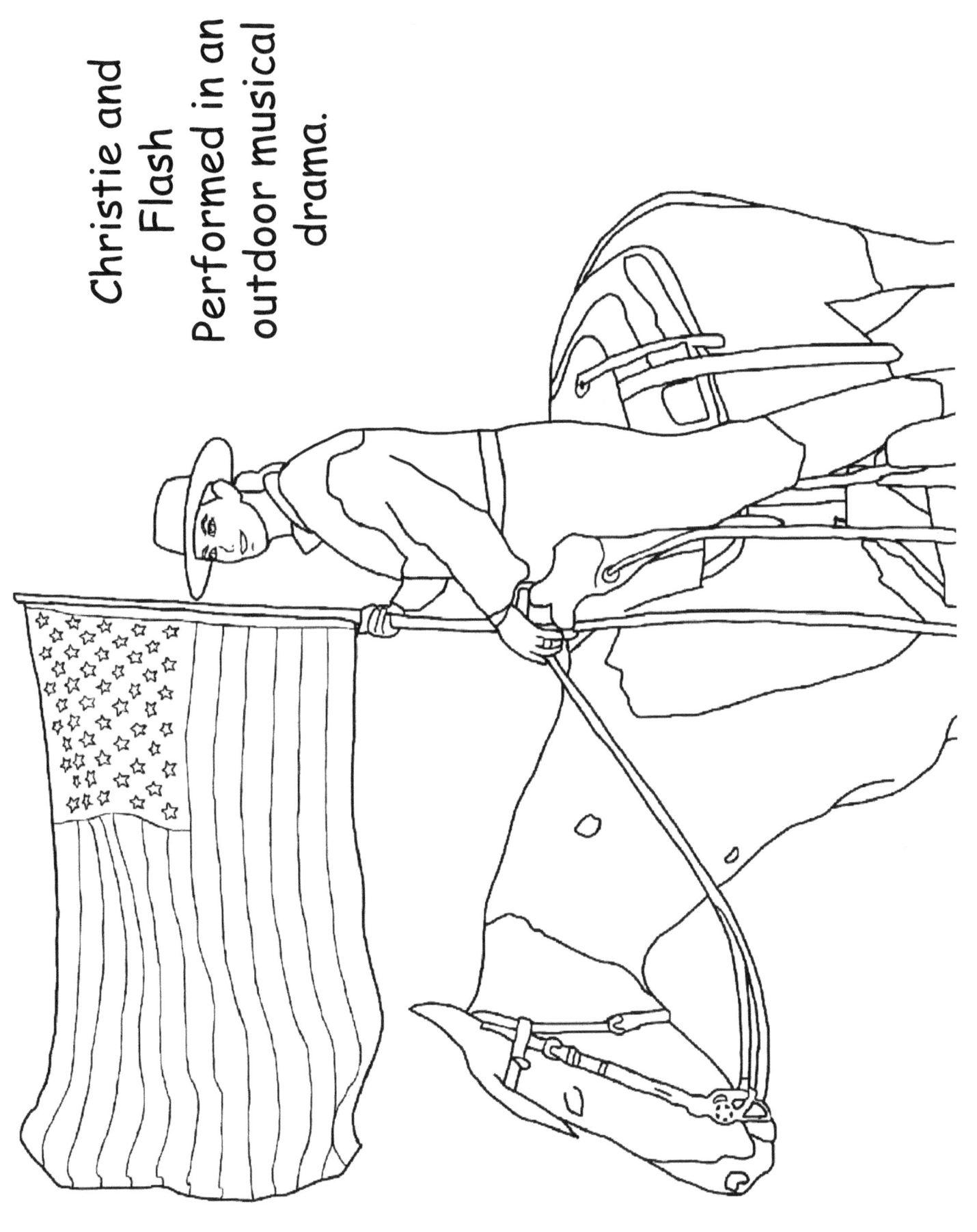

Christie and Flash
Performed in an outdoor musical drama.

A POEM ABOUT ME

Flash
Brave. Smart. Hard-working. Spotted.
Son of a Tennessee Walker.
Lover of Hay.
Who feels happy in my pasture.
Who needs more hay.
Who gives all that I can.
Who fears noises.
Who would like to see my friends.
Resident of the great state of Texas!
A Rescue Horse.

WRITE A POEM ABOUT YOU

Your first name…
Four descriptive traits that describe you…
Sibling of, or son/daughter of…
Lover of …
Who feels…
Who needs…
Who gives…
Who fears…
Who would like to see…
Resident of (your city)…
Your last name…

Write a poem about you on the back of this page.

MEET FLASH

Flash is a rescue horse who was adopted from a horse sanctuary. He is a registered Tennessee Walker. At birth he was given the name Snake Creek Rooster.

Christie is his owner and trainer. Flash was terrified of noises, but Christie worked with him almost every day so that he could perform on stage in an outdoor musical drama. He learned to stand perfectly still with music, lights flashing, dancers, and fireworks.

FLASH'S FUN FACTS

All horses belong to the genus Equus. This group also includes donkeys, zebras, and mules. All equids have long ears, hoofed feet, flowing tails, and a mane on the upper part of their neck.

Horses have the biggest eyes of all mammals. Because their eyes are located on the side of the head, and because the eyes bulge out so far, the horse has a huge range of vision.

A horse's ears can reveal a lot. If they're laid back, it could mean fear or anger. Ears that are up and forward mean the animal is alert, responsive, and aware of his surroundings. If your horse is relaxed and listening his ears are up and wide-spaced.

A horse and a rider can do more together, moving as one, than either can accomplish on their own.

No other symbol in the animal kingdom has inspired as much artistic works, poetry, or literature as the horse. It is the most written about animal.

Turn to the next page to write a story about a horse.

A DAY WITH FLASH

Flash escapes his pen and shows up at your school! Horses are always hungry, so he'll have to eat in the cafeteria with you and he will want to join you at recess. Write a story about what Flash can eat for lunch and his day at your school:

_____
_____
_____
_____
_____
_____
_____
_____
_____
_____
_____
_____
_____
_____
_____
_____
_____
_____

Christie is saddling up Flash to ride in the canyon. What all does Flash need?

```
                    T B
                    U B
                P I A Q
                C U W B
              B O T R Z H
              E W L B R I
T E L U G X C N V Y F R I X S E O H S L
H N D I E C D C G F R M U T O O Y B R O
  S A D D L E M J U T Q U S S H T E K
    J Y X U N M P E C P S M H K I I
      J V Y X N K V C Y J B I N J
        Q E W N X O B I Q E S K
      Z Z O A S C D F L T O T Z B
        Z A L L T R P V E L D I R B
      X T B G P R F U P P Q X Z Q P Y
        A Q I C Z A G   O L E A O R R
          S W Y H B D P   M I B F P F G
          S X U Z C         A N Q B L
        B B M G                 P Y F I
        B C                         T T
```

Bridle   Brush

Blanket   Bit

Strap   Saddle

Reins   Shoes

Stirrup

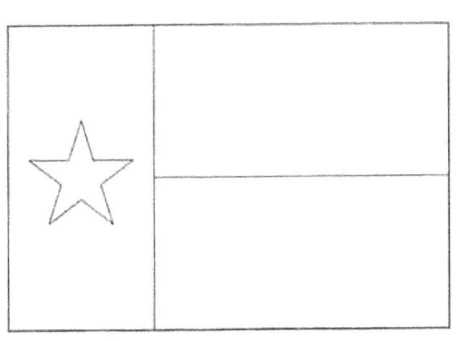

How many words can you make from these letters?

FLASH
THE RESCUE HORSE

_____

_____

_____

_____

_____

_____

_____

_____

_____

This is Jelepe!

Flash Crossword Puzzle

ACROSS
1   Flash was very _____ in the summertime
2   Flash's birth name is Snake _____ Rooster
5   What does Flash ride in when he is not walking?
7   Flash and his group of horses are called a _____
8   Dove Creek Ranch and Equine Rescue is a _____
10 Sometimes, Flash can be _____
11 What is Flash afraid of?
12 What does flash wear on his feet?

DOWN
1   When Flash was adopted, he found a new _____
2   Flash's human is named _____
3   Flash lives in the state of _____
4   Flash and Christie carred a _____ over the Canyon
6   When Christie found Flash, she _____ him
9   In the winter, Flash likes rolling in the _____

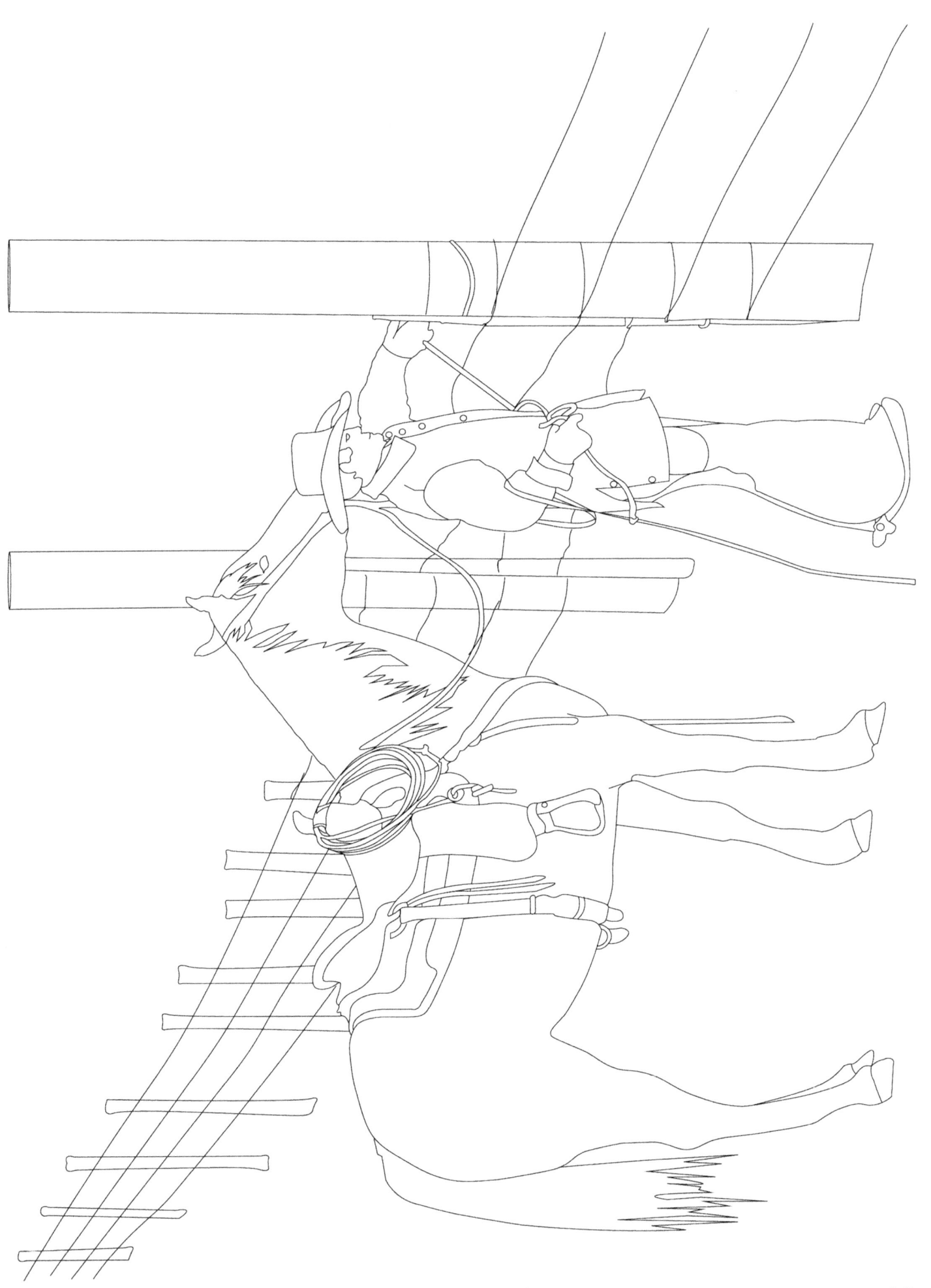

THE DOG

One day on the way to recess, you see a stray dog hanging around the playground. Some of your friends yelled at him to go away. "Go home!" they shouted. You walked closer and the dog said, "Can you help me?"

Write a story about the talking dog.

Dot - to - Dot

Start at Number 1

Draw a horse in the barn and color this page

Crack the picture code puzzle to answer the riddle

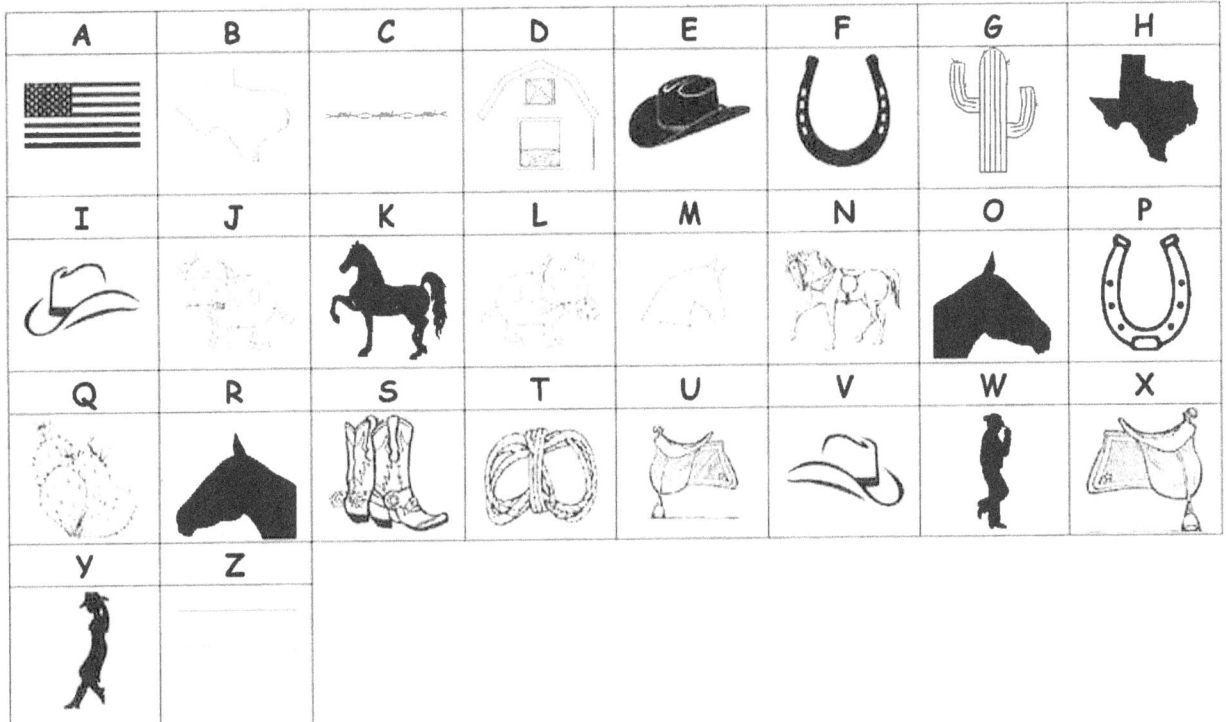

How do you catch a loose horse?

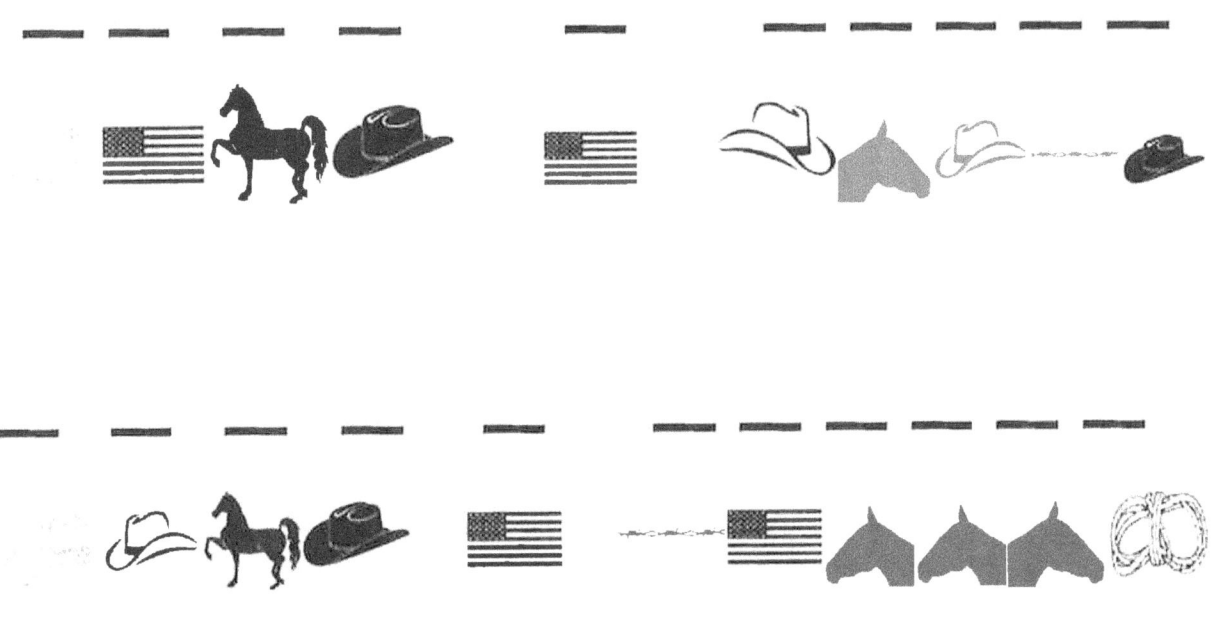

How many horse colors can you find?

```
A K O O T N I P S Y
Y P V E L P P A D I
S I P O P D X I B C
M U W A A K E H S H
Y U M B L A C K M E
T E K M O O D V C S
F P R P M B O F V T
Z Y Z G I E L S J N
B R O W N N U P A U
P K F R O I F G W T
```

Appaloosa   Black   Brown
Buckskin   Chestnut   Dapple
Grey   Palomino   Pinto

AMUSEMENT PARK

You and your friends are having a fun day at the amusement park. Right at closing time, one of your friends realized he had left his jacket on the fence next to the Ferris wheel. Everyone hurried back to help find the jacket, but you did not make it back to the front entrance before they locked the gates and left. You are hungry and tired and there is no way out! Write a story about how you survived the night in the amusement park.

_____
_____
_____
_____
_____
_____
_____
_____
_____
_____
_____
_____
_____
_____
_____
_____
_____
_____
_____

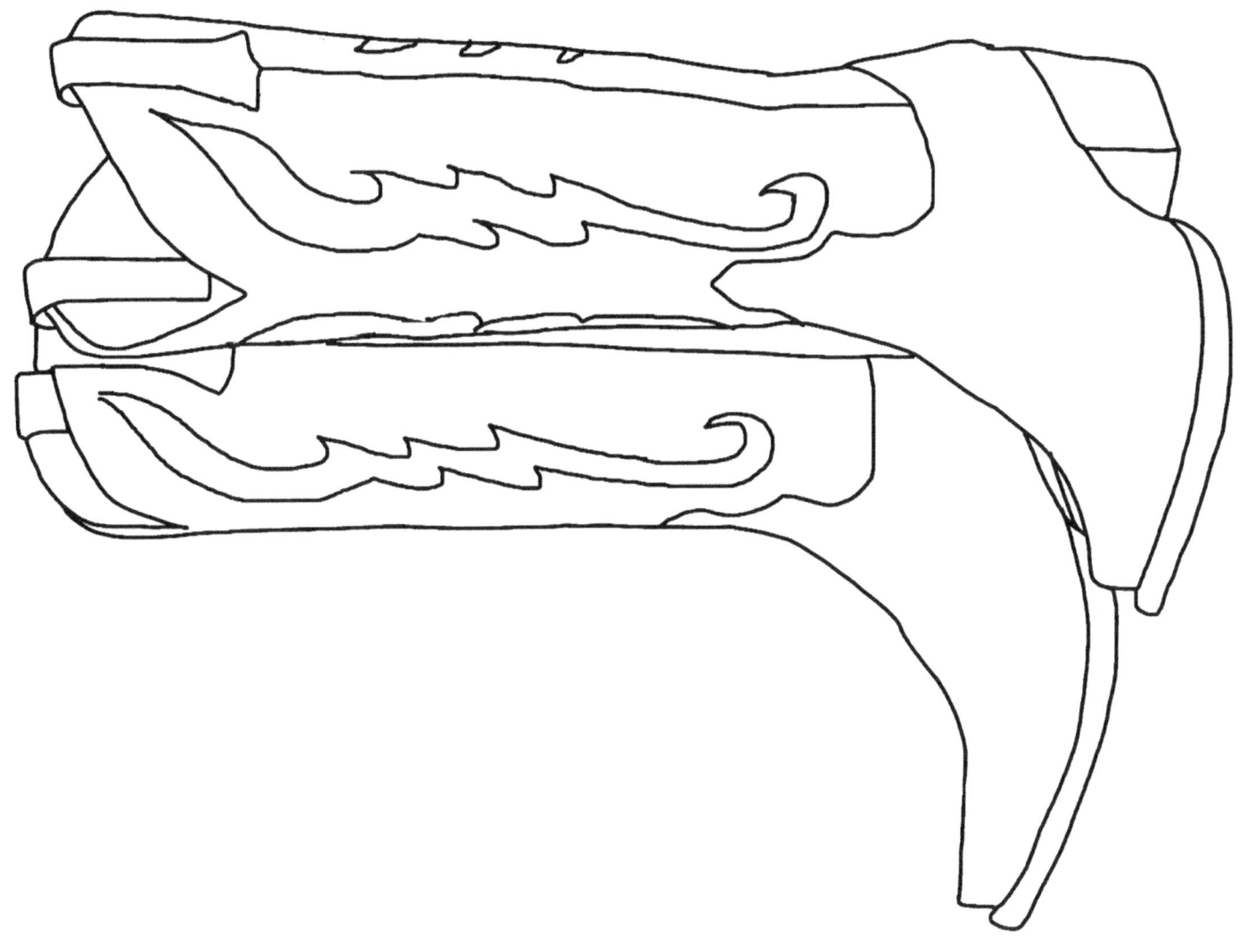

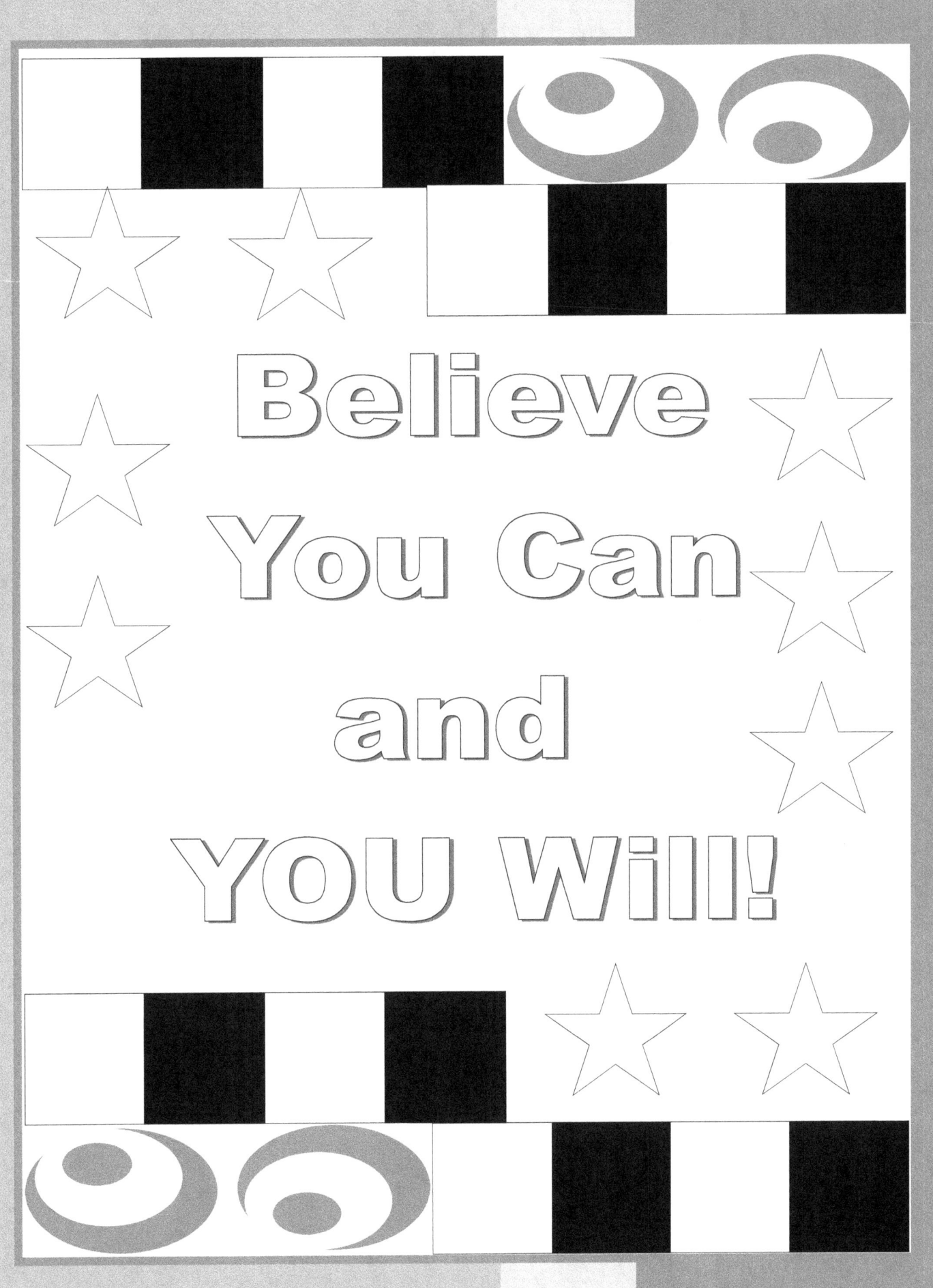

Can you find those words?

```
P L S T I A G Q R U
A O W Y C O S Y E V
M G L R D E U P T K
B C C L Q E R F N D
L H S R A B M V A M
E D Q B D G F M C E
G N I D N U O P B S
M A P E T S E D I S
V D W H C E X O J H
P S T O R T X O F Z
```

Amble   Canter   FoxTrot
Gaits   Gallop   Pounding
Sidestep

The Great State of TEXAS!

You have a new classmate who just moved here from New York City and has never seen a horse before. Write a story about what you will tell your new friend about owning a horse.

_____
_____
_____
_____
_____
_____
_____
_____
_____
_____
_____
_____
_____
_____
_____
_____
_____

Flash lives in Texas!

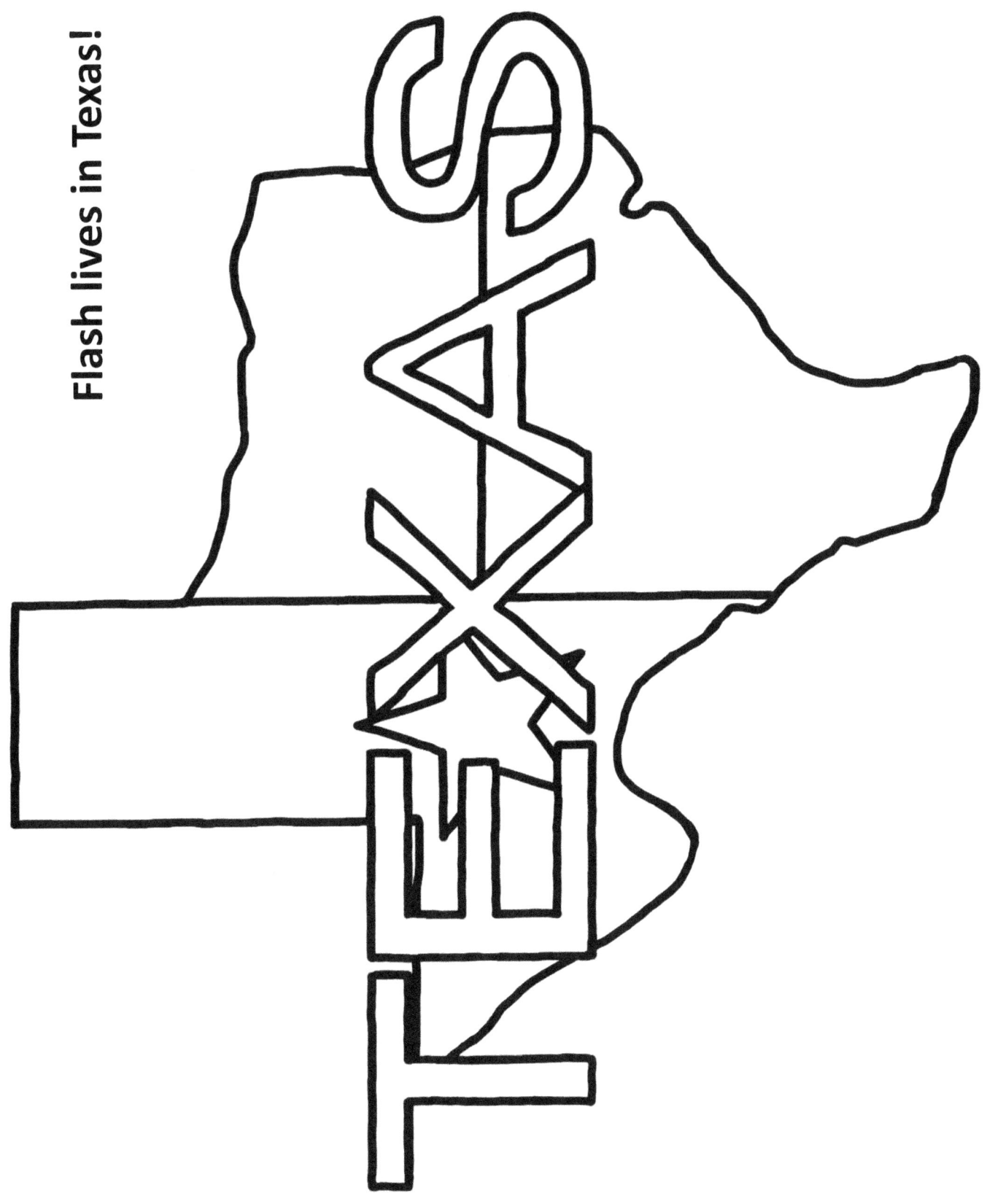

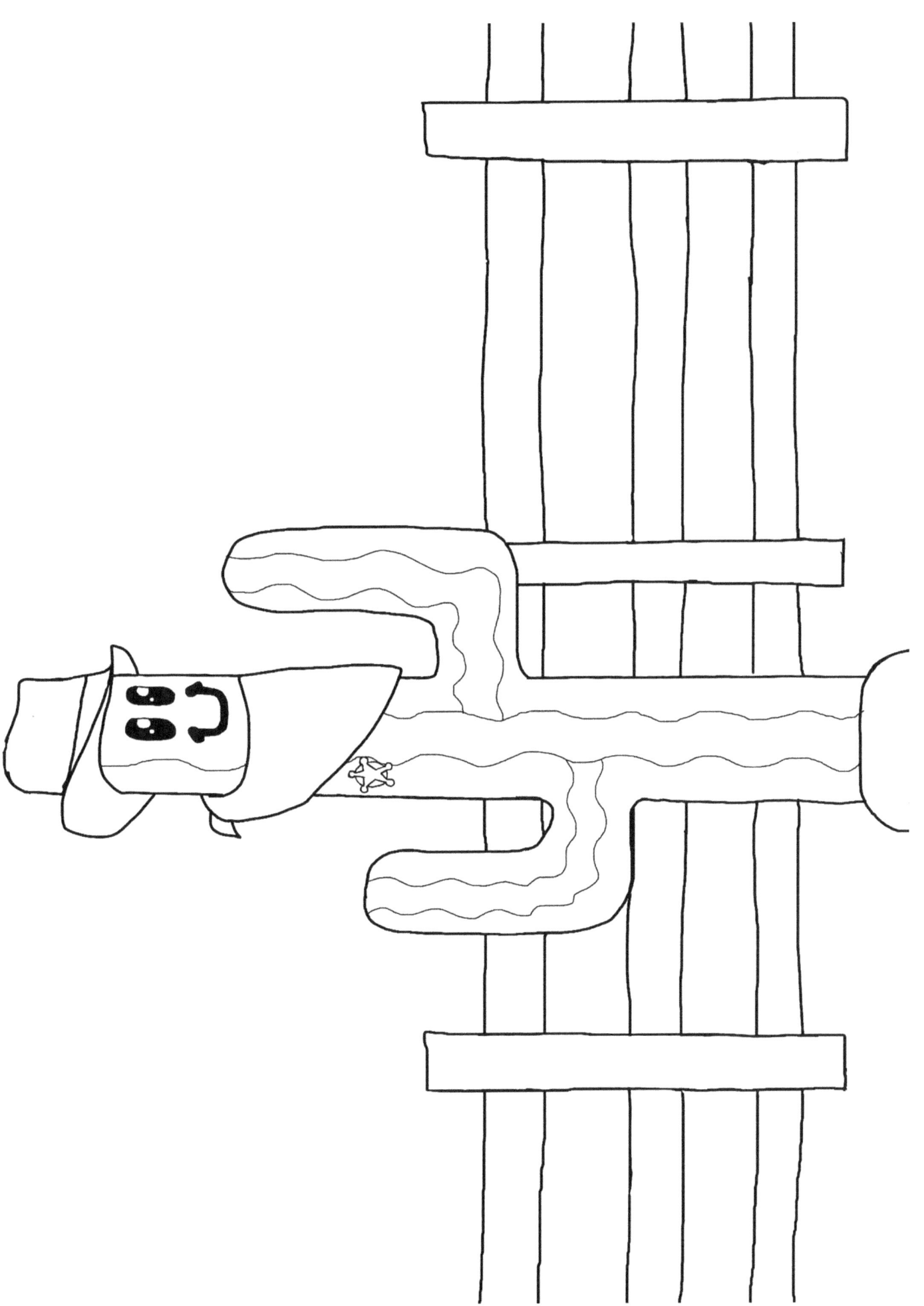

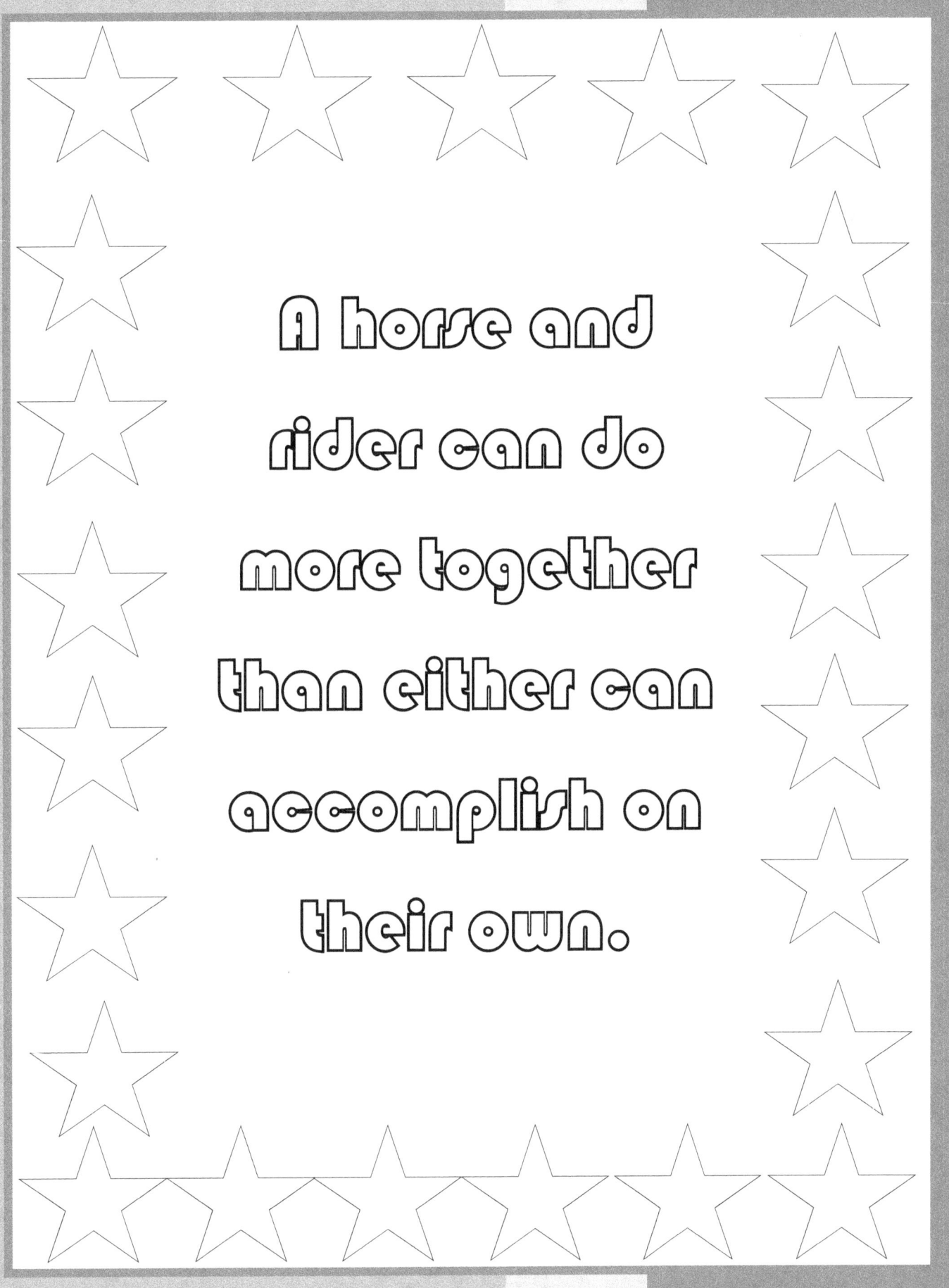

A horse and rider can do more together than either can accomplish on their own.

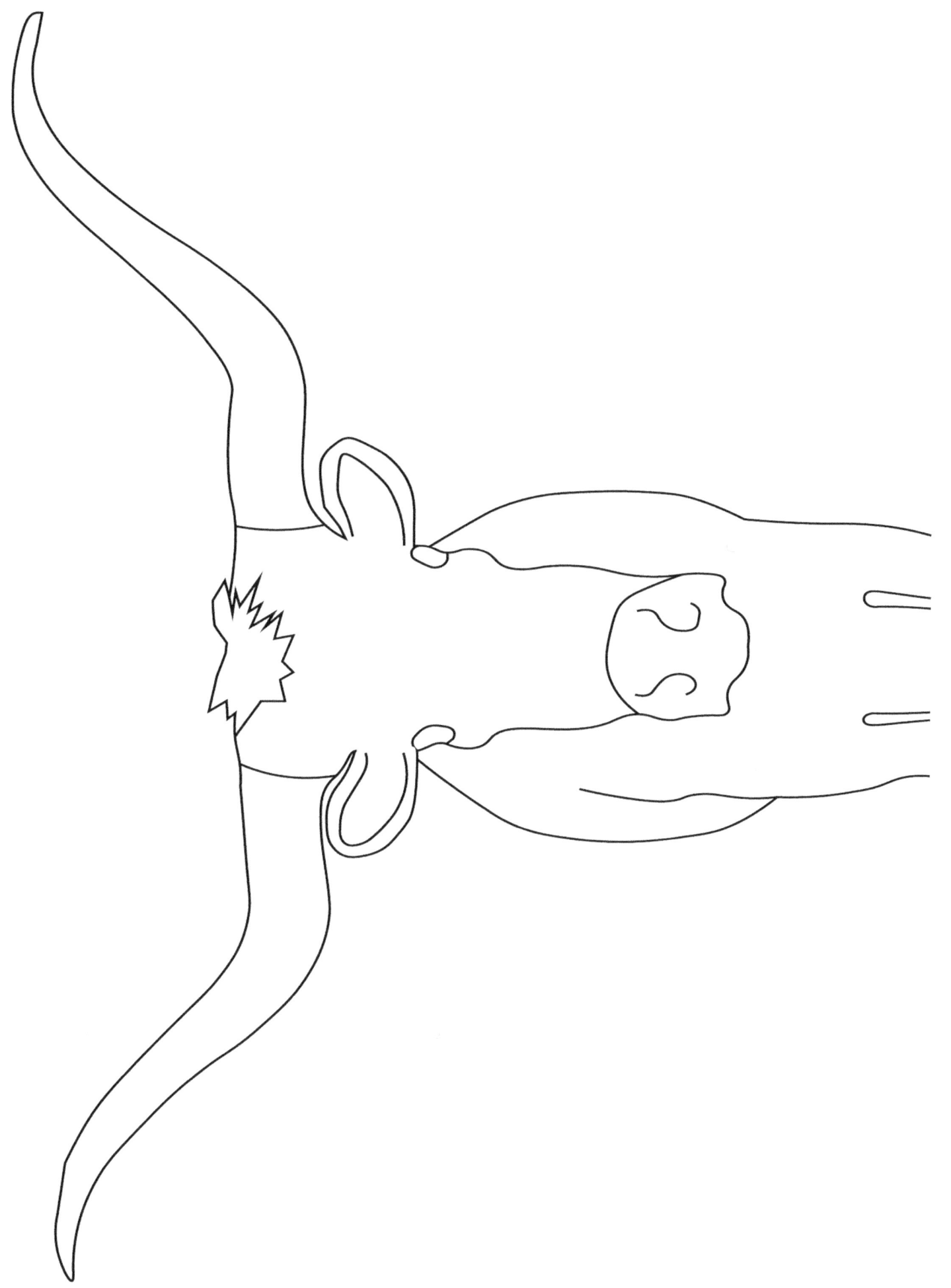

Crack the code with Flash's symbols!

A	B	C	D	E	F	G	H
flag	Texas	barbed wire	barn	hat	horseshoe	cactus	Texas
I	J	K	L	M	N	O	P
hat	horse	horse			horse	horse head	horseshoe
Q	R	S	T	U	V	W	X
cactus	horse head	boots	rope	saddle	hat	cowgirl	saddle
Y	Z						
cowgirl	Texas flag						

Flash is a....

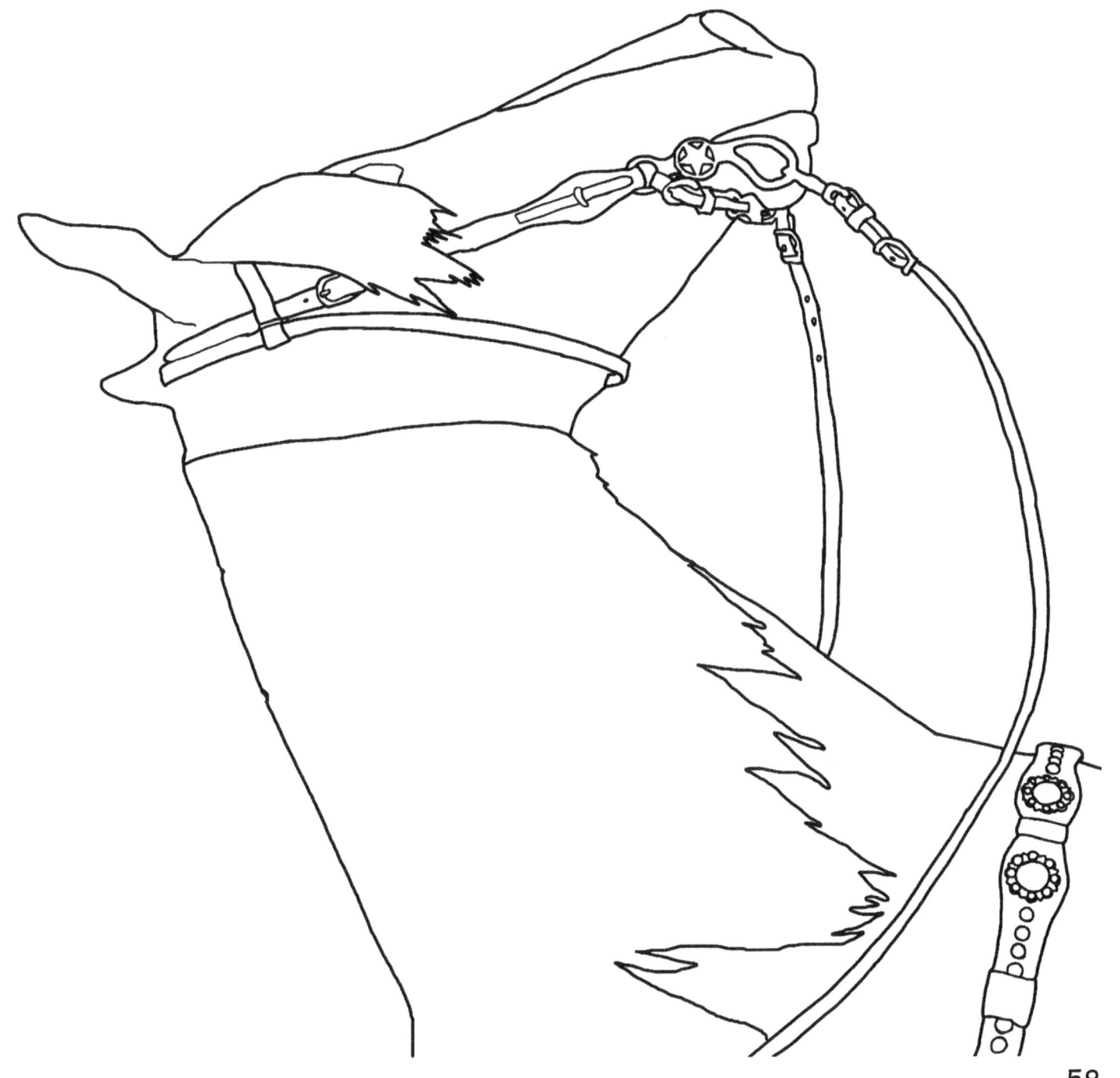

Crack the code with Flash's symbols!

A	B	C	D	E	F	G	H
flag	Texas	barbed wire	barn	cowboy hat	horseshoe	cactus	Texas

I	J	K	L	M	N	O	P
hat	horse	rearing horse	horse	horse	horse w/saddle	horse head	horseshoe

Q	R	S	T	U	V	W	X
cactus	horse head	boots	rope	saddle	hat	cowgirl	saddle

Y	Z
cowgirl	Texas flag

Flash is a….

T E N N E S S E E

W A L K E R

It's time to saddle up. What do you need?

```
T K C H A P S L Y T H U C K M
E P Y B R I D L E L A S S O O
K R N Y Q E A G S G W R I W C
N Z O V W O Y S P V X C S X I
A V I V A H V R F C P X R W N
L L A T S D A E H T O B N Q C
B H J Q A O L R M Q C U O Y H
B R L N D F S O R S O G G I T
V Y Y A D E S M I G T A M V T
G B I D L W E A S O L R K Y A
K O Y U E D C K X K T R A N F
H B I T I Q Q C Q R C L R P U
B V M M N H Z A C F T N E N L
C Q L C F M S H U M C M R A E
B E F C G R O J L P H Y R Y D
```

Bit   Blanket   Bridle
Chaps   Cinch   Hackamore
HeadStall   Lasso   Lead
Strap   Saddle

How many words can you rhyme with

FLASH

_____
_____
_____
_____
_____
_____
_____
_____
_____

www.ingramcontent.com/pod-product-compliance
Lightning Source LLC
Chambersburg PA
CBHW051354070526
44584CB00025B/3759